YOUR KNOWLEDGE HAS VALUE

AF131189

- We will publish your bachelor's and master's thesis, essays and papers

- Your own eBook and book - sold worldwide in all relevant shops

- Earn money with each sale

Upload your text at www.GRIN.com and publish for free

GRIN :)

Bibliographic information published by the German National Library:

The German National Library lists this publication in the National Bibliography; detailed bibliographic data are available on the Internet at http://dnb.dnb.de .

Imprint:

Copyright © 2012 GRIN Verlag, Open Publishing GmbH
Print and binding: Books on Demand GmbH, Norderstedt Germany
ISBN: 978-3-668-15548-0

This book at GRIN:

http://www.grin.com/en/e-book/231266/import-substitution-industrialization-and-the-effects-of-globalization

Stephen Gumboh

Import Substitution Industrialization and the Effects of Globalization on the Manufacturing Sector in Zambia

GRIN Publishing

GRIN - Your knowledge has value

Since its foundation in 1998, GRIN has specialized in publishing academic texts by students, college teachers and other academics as e-book and printed book. The website www.grin.com is an ideal platform for presenting term papers, final papers, scientific essays, dissertations and specialist books.

Visit us on the internet:

http://www.grin.com/

http://www.facebook.com/grincom

http://www.twitter.com/grin_com

Globalization and International Development

Import Substitution Industrialization and the Effects of Globalization on the Manufacturing
Sector in Zambia

Stephen Gumboh
Ministry of Finance
National Policy and Programme Implementation
Lusaka, Zambia

March 2012

Globalization and International Development

Abstract

The paper discusses the essence of the Import Substitution Industrialization (ISI) policy adopted by the Zambian government prior to trade liberalization and the effects of globalization on the growth and development of manufacturing sector thereafter. Specifically, the paper analyses the merits and effectiveness of the ISI policy on the growth of the Zambia industry with particular emphasis on the impact of globalization and trade liberalization on the Zambian manufacturing sector and the government possible measures and instruments necessary to maximize the benefits of globalization.

The paper proves the heavy impact of trade liberalization on the manufacturing sector in peak period of its implementation. As for the import substitution policy and the effects of globalization on the growth and development of manufacturing sector, the paper also cites these among many other factors as major attributes to a greater extent to the failure of the manufacturing sector to perform to expectation over the peak period of trade liberalization. Government policies to cushion itself from the effects of globalization and to revitalize the manufacturing sector are equally proved to have brought about some favorable results despite the many constraints that the sector has had to face over the years of trade liberalization. The paper concludes by emphasizing the need for the government to continue pursuing policy measures strategically focused on the growth of the sector by seriously taking into consideration its backward and forward linkages in the economy.

Keywords: Import Substitution Industrialization, Manufacturing, Globalization, Trade Liberation, Regional Economic Integration.

i

Globalization and International Development

Table of Contents

Abbreviations and Acronyms

AGOA	American Growth Opportunity for Africa
COMESA	Common Market for Eastern and Southern Africa
FNDP	Fifth National Development Plan
FTA	Free Trade Area
GDP	Gross Domestic Product
IMF	International Monetary Fund
ISI	Import Substitution Industrialization
MMD	Movement for Multi-Party Democracy
MFEZ	Multi-Facility Economic Zones
MSME	Micro, Small and Medium Enterprises
SACU	South Africa Customs Union
SADC	Southern Africa Development Community
SNDP	Sixth National Development Plan
UNIP	United National Independence Party
VAT	Value Added Tax

Globalization and International Development

1 Introduction

1.1 Background

In an effort to increase productivity and economic gains within the country, most of the developing countries in the 1980s adopted the Import Substitution Industrialization (ISI) strategy. This strategy was adopted for inward economic growth as remedy to the even increasing poverty levels which were being experienced in most of the developing economies, greatly attributed to the economic structure that existed at the time, mostly dominated by raw agriculture and mining activities without much benefit from international trade. It was this background that formed the basis for the infant-industry argument for national industrialization in most of the developing economies.

However, at the onset of the structural indebtedness of developing economies that arose from ISI related policies, the ISI had to be abandoned by most of the developing nations, Zambia inclusive, in 1990s. This was mostly instigated by International Monetary Fund (IMF) and the World Bank through their structural adjustment programs of market driven liberalization. The structural adjustment programs entailed developing economies embracing globalization by integrating their economies into a single global market open to competition. Negatively, most of the developing nations could not cope with such developments having excessively protected their industries from competition under the "infant- industry argument" which advocated for protective tariffs to enable infant-industries in developing economies to establish themselves inwardly before exposing them to international competitive trade. Zambia as one such developing economy have had to experience both effects of import substitution industrialization and the impact of globalization on most of its economic sectors due to trade liberalization. One such sector heavily impacted was the Manufacturing sector. It was these experiences that formed the essence of the study.

1.2 Statement of the Problem

At independence, Zambia inherited an economy that was heavily dependent on the production of copper, besides other minerals such as lead, zinc and cobalt. Relying on the revenues provided by the lucrative copper prices in the sixties and early seventies, Zambia established an economic structure based on extensive government control over most aspects of the economy. Much of Zambia's emphasis on the development agenda laid on industrial manufacturing activities aimed at processing of raw materials and intermediate goods for local consumption as well as for export. To achieve this development agenda, the government adopted the Import Substitution Industrialization (ISI Strategy aimed at inward diversification of the economy in the production of consumer, intermediate and capital goods.

By adopting the ISI strategy, most of the industrial sectors experienced considerable growth. The manufacturing sector, which was the main focus of the study for example, did "experience growth at considerable rate with its output increasing steadily at an average rate of 14.2 percent per annum in the period 1968 – 1975" (Turok, 1979, p101). The impressive expansion in the industrial manufacturing output in the period was also largely due to the protective measures such as high tariff barriers which were largely offered to government owned local industries. The trend however changed at the advent of the economic crisis in the country after 1975. This was attributed to the decline in copper earnings that made it difficult for the manufacturing industry to cope with the crisis. The crisis made it difficult for the sector to recapitalize itself due to lack of foreign exchange to import most of the inputs required to enhance its productivity. The situation even forced most of the manufacturing industries to cut down their production capacities.

The non-availability of foreign exchange within the manufacturing sector was a serious challenge as it made it difficult for the sector to strive even on the local market. This was despite most of the sector's products being targeted at domestic market without recourse to exports "in line with government policy that restricted the exports of manufactured products" (Gulhati 1989, p23). This meant that the sector had no choice but to strive to sustain its production capacity within the limited foreign exchange available. Due to the economic crisis that the government experienced in the 1990s, it was left with no choice but to undertake fully-fledged trade reforms as an alternative solution. One such solution was to open up the economy to competition as recommended by the IMF and World Bank. It was the opening up of the economy to international competition that brought a lot of challenges to the manufacturing sector. One such challenge was the "loss of large segments on the home market to foreign imports' as a result of cheap imports from the global market" (Chikoti and Mutonga, 2002, p3). The loss of the local market to foreign imports hampered the manufacturing industry from becoming a lead industry for exports.

1.3 Objectives of the Study

The objective of the study was mainly to discuss the essence of the ISI policy adopted by government prior to trade liberalization and the effects of globalization on the growth and development of manufacturing sector in Zambia. Specific objectives of the study were to analyse the merits and effectiveness of the ISI policy on the growth of the Zambia industry with particular emphasis on the manufacturing sector; to analyse the impact of globalization on the Zambian economy; to analyse the effects of trade liberalization on the manufacturing sector and the effectiveness of measures which were undertaken by government to cushion the effects of globalization and finally to provide some options to government on some possible measures and instruments necessary for the country to maximize the benefits of globalization.

1.4 Methodology of the Study

Considering the limitations of the study, the study had to be limited to desk research. Most of the vital documentation were analysed in line with the study objectives. To verify data, various stakeholder institutions were contacted and interviews conducted on the authenticity of the data and possible interventions by government on its quest to enhance the benefits of globalization. Among the key stakeholder institutions were the Central Statistics Office, Ministry of Finance and National Planning, Ministry of Labour and Social Security, Manufacturing Association of Zambia, Economics Association of Zambia, Zambia Federation of Employers and the Zambia Chamber of Commerce.

2 Review of literature

2.1 Import Substitution Industrialization

Import substitution industrialization (ISI) from the layman point of view meant the replacement of foreign imports with domestic production. This implied "the reduction of dependency on foreign products by replacing them with the locally produced ones" (Osei-Hwedie, 2005, p1). By adopting the ISI strategy, imported goods from the developed economies were to be foregone in preference to those to be produced internally. The essence of the ISI was to enhance the development of the local market to the level of self-sufficiency in the production of the goods suitable and at the dictate of the local market. Most of the ISI policies were premised on the infant industry argument where the local industries were made to operate under protectionist trade policies to enable them to develop inwardly.

The protectionist trade policies were meant to enable "infant" industries to develop first to the level of accumulating enough capital and sufficient industrial knowledge to enable them to compete favorably on the world market. The idea of pursuing inward-looking protectionist trade policies such as imposing high tariffs on imported goods were mostly aimed at deterring local consumers from demanding more of the imports at the expense of the locally produced goods. By implication, import substitution did not therefore mean import elimination but as a means of providing opportunities to the country in its industrialization efforts. This was mainly in the solicitation of importation of essential goods such as petroleum, chemicals, and the raw materials necessary for its industrial production. In other worlds, the real objective of import substitution was not therefore to only trade but also to enhance the local industries to the level of adding value to the local products to make them competitive internationally.

2.2 Infant – Industry Argument

As alluded to earlier, Government protection tendencies of the local industries was conceptualized from the infant –industry argument which advocated for protectionist trade policies for purpose of allowing new and undeveloped local industries to establish themselves first before subjecting them to international competition. The argument bordered on the notion that an infant industry did not have the ability to compete with mature established industries due to its smallness in terms of economics of scale and therefore had to be large enough to harvest the economics of scale in production to become competitive. The temporary shielding of infant domestic industries from severe competition gave them the opportunity to develop and become efficient producers to compete effectively with more mature and efficient foreign industries. Taking into consideration the historical differences in levels of economic development between domestic and foreign industries, it therefore followed that the provision of protection to infant – industries would correct the perceived misallocation of world resources in favour of well-established and technically developed foreign industries.

Historically, it was found that even among the new industrialized countries, protective measures on infant –industries had to be put in place before fully exposing them to international competition. For example, Great Britain, which in the mid –nineteenth century, was the leading industrial country made it difficult for Germany to compete with its older and more established British industries (Sorderstein,1980,p196). In spite of having a free market economy, Germany had to ensure that her local industry was fully developed in production efficiency before letting it to stand up to the British industry on the international market. The south-east Asian economies such as that of Japan and South Korea were purported to have recorded a lot of inward successes in its industry development through the protectionist tendencies over its industries by successfully promoting steel and car production and cooperative efforts in basic research – especially in electronics (World Development Report, 1987, p70). These economies' successful performance suggested that intelligent government intervention in industry by offering protection, promoted specific industrial activities to enhance industrial productivity.

2.3 Trade Liberalization

The argument on trade liberalization laid on its effect on infant domestic industries. The argument was that a liberalized trade regime would lead to a substantial rise in the importation of goods and services at the expense of the local products. The issue was that foreign products which were presumed to be of high quality and cheaper than the local products would therefore lead to an increase in their importation as consumers' demand for them increased. Consequently, this would lead the demand for local products to decline, eventually leading to domestic industries losing market to foreign industries which were usually competitively favored in international trade due export subsidies offered to them to boast their exports as a way of expanding their international market. Without government putting in place appropriate protective measures, this would have had devastating effects on the local industry as continued increase in imports of the subsidized foreign products into the domestic economy would not only make the local industry to loss market but equally fold up in the long run.

There was also the argument that unfair competition in international trade had had a negative effect on manufacturing sector employment. This was because in situations of unfair competition, the perception was that the levels of unemployment in the domestic economy would essentially increase once local industries fold up in the face of stiff competition with technologically advanced financial resource endowed foreign industries. In the long run, the economy would be reduced from a producing nation to a market for foreign manufactured goods. This was especially eminent when the free market economic policies were adopted by an economy in transition from government controlled to a free market system without accompanying foreign investments and establishment of new industries to contain the rising unemployment levels.

2.4   Structure of the Zambian Industry

Notably, the Zambia industrial sector had been, prior to liberalization, dominated by the parastatal sector with the government owning major shares in most of the key industrial units. The protection of the parastatals dominated the industrial sector and consequently this dominance stifled competition and initiative as most of the industrial units which were created had no rival units to offer credible competition. It was this lack of credible competition that resulted in low quality products and imposition of high prices as most of the parastatals become effective monopolies. On the other hand, lack of initiatives and innovations in running these parastatals brought about inefficiencies into the industry as most of industrial units were not able to initiate ways and means of how there were to improve their production techniques. The problem was further compounded by the political bureaucratic structures that existed and allowed no independence in the running of these industrial units. The lack of initiatives and innovations in the industrial units plunged them into economic crisis. Ultimately this led to declining capacity utilization in most industries and many of them become inefficient.

Despite the economic crisis and the industrial inefficiencies the country was experiencing, the government vigorously went ahead with its industrial programmmes. It was not until the gravity of the crisis was heavily felt that some projects such as the Iron and steel industry which was to have been established in the country and planned to resume operations by 1981 had to be abandoned. The government policy framework of ISI of tariff barriers to nurture the local infant industries could not even help to resuscitate declining industrial sector. As the economic crisis worsened, government's efforts to reform the industrial sector in the late 1980 proved unsuccessful. This was evidently clear as most of the parastatal industrial units found themselves with no capacity to help in the diversification of the economy to the country's national comparative advantage. The ushering into government of the Movement for Multi-party Democracy (MMD) in 1991 brought dramatic change to country's economic policy framework.

2.5 Genesis of the Economic Crisis in Zambia

The oil shock of 1973 coupled with the decline in copper proceeds marked the genesis of the economic crisis in Zambia. With the increase in oil import bill and declining copper export earnings meant a resource constraint in the economy as foreign exchange became scarce. This was further worsened by the fact that policy framework of government encouraged consumption at the expense of savings and investment. The policy equally discriminated against the development of the indigenous resource base particularly agriculture. Consumption was heavily import intensive and consumer subsidies became wide spread. Despite the downturn of the economy, the policy regime was maintained and intensified.

To offset the revenue downturns due to the fall in the copper prices, the government resorted to heavy foreign borrowings. This led to severe build up of foreign debt. From 1982 up to 1992, the country had already entered into an acute economic and financial crisis, with most industries operating far below full capacity utilization levels.

2.6 Zambia's Experience of Globalization and its Effects on the Industrial Sector

Zambia's experience of globalization could be traced back to the time at the time the economy was liberalized in line with the economic reforms undertaken by government at the initiation of the IMF and World Bank. This followed the ushering of the Movement for Multi-party Democracy (MMD) which took over political power from the United National Independence Party (UNIP) in 1991.

At the accession to power, the MMD government made many dramatic changes to the policy framework. In its reform agenda, the MMD government mandated itself to reform the economy from the one of interventionist to a free market economy with significant reduction in the role of government. Free market economy was favoured as the most plausible to the economic crisis that the country was experiencing at the time. In their campaign manifesto, the MMD made specific proposals to reform the economy which included privatization of virtually all the entire parastatal sector and restructuring of the utilities that were to remain in public ownership.

In its 1992 budget, the MMD government made a determined start by putting up comprehensive reforms aimed at encouraging exports, liberalizing the economy and privatizing most of the parastatal sector. Most importantly the privatization programme involved the withdrawal of protective measures to the local industry that characterized the era of the UNIP government. The local industry was made to globally compete with foreign companies in terms of product development and marketing.

The opening up of the economy to competition in 1992 signified the entry of the country onto the global stage. It was at this point that the country started to experience globalization in terms of trade, finance and information sharing within an integrated single global market. The integration of national economies meant opening the way for the transnational expansion of economic activities beyond national borders. This was evidently clear in production of goods and services, marketing, financing, communications and labour mobility.

3   Study Findings and Comments

3.1   The Impact of Globalization on the Zambian Economy

The study found that the Zambian economy was one of those developing economies that had not greatly benefited from globalization due to its failure to meet the minimum basic requirements of globalization. According to Mulungushi (2005, p150), these minimum basic requirements included "information, knowledge, technology and networking which were regarded as key pillars and ingredients for a nation to effectively benefit from globalization". These elements were found to be closely related to economic growth and development in terms of productivity. Arguably, the study found that the country had been trying to meet theses minimum basic infrastructure requirements especially in energy, road, and telecommunications sectors. These infrastructures were regard as essential to the development the economy in its pursuit to drive benefits from globalization.

In analyzing the effects of globalization on the performance of the economy, the study found that data in terms of country's Gross Domestic Product (GDP) and per capita income, experienced a declining trend in the early periods of globalization, illustrating the point that

8

country was experiencing marginalization in capital flows, information and technological advancement of globalization. This was despite the country's effort to put in place some measures such as the liberalization of the economy in trying to benefit from globalization.

The other major factor was lack of access to international market despite its efforts to focus on export growth to fully benefit from globalization. This was as result of the country Zambia with its small population had most of its people impoverished making it difficult for them to absorb all the expanded domestic input and as such needed to find external markets for most of its products. The issue of expanding the market was critical to country where the smallness of domestic market made it difficult to support large scale production because of low purchasing power as a result of poverty. This was found as a reason why the economy experienced rapid deterioration in the nineties which was partly because of the failure of the local industries to expand into both local and international markets.

Notwithstanding the adoption of import substitution strategy by the UNIP government, the limitation of the markets and inability of the local industries to penetrate international markets was found to have caused its failure to meet the intended objectives. This was attributed to the lack of improved and efficient communication network in highly deregulated markets for a country to enter foreign markets. This meant that the country's international capital could not operate freely across the national borders. The choice was for the country to embrace total liberalization of the economy to benefit from globalization. This was because the ability to mobilize capital from anywhere and invest it anywhere through various instruments such as capital markets supported by information systems and networks was presumed to be at the centre of globalization. The issue was that the benefits of globalization resulted in situations there was the search for new markets and internationalized production. The country's failure to attract foreign investment despite embarking on the liberalization course clearly proved the assumption that the country had not been able to benefit much from globalization as manifested in the levels of inequality and poverty levels that the country was experiencing.

3.2 Regional Economic Integration and Zambia Manufacturing Sector Growth

The country's active participation in the global and regional trading arrangements under AGOA, COMESA and SADC brought with it positive effects on the manufacturing sector growth. Under the AGOA facility, for example, the country's exports showed an increase although the majority of the products were through third-countries. As for the manufacturers, these have at least continued to benefit from the COMESA-Free Trade Area (FTA) and the SADC Trade Protocol.

In the case of SADC, the study found that the country has been able to benefit mainly on the exports of textile products under the South Africa Customs Union (SACU) – Malawi, Mozambique, Tanzania and Zambia textile arrangement, which give duty free market access into the South African market. In addition, exports of sugar, copper rods and copper cables increased because of the implementation of the SADC Trade Protocol. The SADC Trade Protocol gave these products duty free market access into the South African market. The growth in the basic metal products sub-sector, for example, equally benefited in increased exports of copper rods and copper cables to South Africa, under the SADC Trade Protocol.

Further, the study found that the country's entry into the Free Trade Agreement brought benefits to some industries that utilize imported inputs from within the COMESA region as a result of the removal of duties on raw materials. This was as a result of raw materials from COMESA countries benefiting from the zero rate tariffs making locally manufactured goods to become more competitively priced. This was despite the challenge for the sector mainly from non-FTA sourced inputs. This was because statistically about 50 percent of manufacturing inputs were found to be sourced from non-COMESA countries. This meant that goods with a higher non-COMESA sourced input element were found to be less competitive on both the domestic and foreign market. This enabled the local manufacturing industry to adequately prepare for the challenge of competing in a broadened export oriented market environment.

3.3 Pre -Trade liberalization Performance of the Manufacturing Sector

The study found that the manufacturing sector's performance had evolved over time despite its recognition as a provider of backward and forward linkages in accelerating growth in agriculture and other natural resource-based industries such as mining and tourism. The study found that the sector recorded significant growth in the period 1964 to 1973 when copper prices were high. It was the high copper prices that enabled government to adopt the ISI strategy which facilitated the establishment of local industries. These local industries were mostly established to provide backup services to mining activities and other related sectors.

In the same period, the study found that the share of manufacturing to total GDP averaged 20 percent per annum while its contribution to formal employment ranged between 40 to 45 percent (Central Statistics Office, 2012). However, the trend changed at the advent of the economic crisis in the country after 1975 after the decline in copper earnings that made it difficult for the manufacturing industry to cope. This was the period when the sector found it difficult to recapitalize it due to lack of foreign exchange needed for importation of most of the inputs required for its production. This eventually forced the sector to cut down its production capacity. The trend continued throughout the 1980s up to the time of trade liberalization in 1992.

Detailed analysis of the performance of the manufacturing sector prior to trade liberalization in 1992, found that the sector's performance showed a downward trend in respond to the fell of the copper prices and increase in oil prices experienced in the mid-1970s, causing most of the manufacturing subsectors such as those for chemicals, rubber and basic metals and metal products that were directly linked to copper proceeds to experience low capacity utilization coupled with high production costs. The decreasing capacity utilization was attributed to the shortage of inputs due to the non-availability of foreign exchange as a result of protectionist measures that made most of the manufacturing industries not to compete effectively on the international market. Issues of inefficiencies in the management of the manufacturing industries due to political interferences were also brought to the surface. The table 1.1 and 1.2 below signified variations in the performance of the manufacturing sector prior to and at the onset of trade liberalization in the period 1989 to 1995.

Table 1.1: Manufacturing Sector GDP at Constant (1977) Prices, 1989 -1995 (K' Million)

Subsector	1989	1990	1991	1992	1993	1994	1995
Food, Beverages and Tobacco	241.7	268.8	284.3	357.1	347.3	335.2	336.9
Textile, and leather industries	79.2	83.4	72.9	70.3	50.2	47.1	41
Wood and wood products	9.4	10.4	11.9	11.4	12.0	9.9	8.6
Paper and Paper products	36.3	33.9	33.4	32.5	31.9	32.1	22.5
Chemicals, Rubber and Plastic products	36.4	38.1	38.6	35.6	37.4	28.8	25.1
Non-metallic mineral products	28.2	32.8	22.9	22.1	20.1	13.8	14.6
Basic metal products	2.4	2.2	2.2	2.5	2.5	2.3	2.2
Fabricated metal products	100.2	103.3	106.7	109.4	89.1	70.7	74.9
Other Manufacturing	10.3	13.8	13.7	16.4	14.7	13.2	12.4
Total	544.1	586.7	586.6	657.3	605.2	553.1	538.2
Real GDP	2,224.20	2,213.50	2,212.70	2,174.40	2322.2	2121.9	2029.9

Source: Economic Reports 1994/1995/1996, Central Statistics Office

Table 1.2: Changes in the Manufacturing Sector GDP, 1989 -1995

Subsector	1989	1990	1991	1992	1993	1994	1995
Food, Beverages and Tobacco		11.2	5.8	25.6	(2.7)	(3.5)	0.5
Textile, and leather industries		5.3	(12.6)	(3.6)	(28.6)	(6.2)	(13.0)
Wood and wood products		10.6	14.4	(4.2)	5.3	(17.5)	(13.1)
Paper and Paper products		(6.6)	(1.5)	(2.7)	(1.8)	0.6	(29.9)
Chemicals, Rubber and Plastic products		4.7	1.3	(7.8)	5.1	(23.0)	(12.8)
Non-metallic mineral products		16.3	(30.2)	(3.5)	(9.0)	(31.3)	5.8
Basic metal products		(8.3)	-	13.6	-	(8.0)	(4.3)
Fabricated metal products		3.1	3.3	2.5	(18.6)	(20.7)	5.9
Other Manufacturing		34.0	(0.7)	19.7	(10.4)	(10.2)	(6.1)
Manufacturing Sector Growth		7.8	(0.0)	12.1	(7.9)	(8.6)	(2.7)
Manufacturing Sector Contribution to GDP Growth	24.5	26.5	26.5	30.2	26.1	26.1	26.5

Source: Self Computations

The data in the table showed that prior to trade been liberalized in 1992, the manufacturing sector experienced a lot of fluctuations in its performance in terms of its output growth and contribution to GDP. For instance, in 1990, the sector's contribution to real total GDP showed a marginal increase of only 2.0 percent to 26.5 percent when compared to the 1989 figure of 24.5 percent. On the other hand, the output growth in the manufacturing sector increased by 7.8 per cent in 1990 but declined to zero per cent in 1991 and only to increase again by 12.1 in 1992. The manufacturing sector contribution to GDP however remained constant at 26.5 per cent in 1990 and 1991. The 1991 negative performance of the sector was attributed to uncertainties that surrounded the sector in an election year.

In the same period, the performance of the manufacturing subsector varied. For instance the performance in 1990 showed an increase in output growth accounted mainly by the favorable sub-sector performance in the food, beverages and tobacco (11.2 percent), textile and leather (5.3 percent), wood and wood products (5.0 percent), chemicals, rubber and plastics products

(16.3 percent), fabricated metal products (3.1 percent) and other manufacturing (34.0 percent). Only the paper and paper products and basic metal products registered negative output growth of 6.6 percent and 8.3 percent respectively.

As for 1991, the manufacturing subsector performance equally varied in their contribution to output growth. Positive output growth recorded under the food, beverages and tobacco subsector of 5.8 percent, a decline of 5.4 percent from the 11.8 percent registered in 1990. The wood and wood products subsector recorded a 14.4 percent output growth, an improvement of 3.8 percent from the 10.6 percent registered in 1990. The fabricated metal products subsector also recorded a minimal increase of only 0.2 percent from the 3.1 percent in 1990 to 3.2 percent in 1991. All the other subsectors recorded negative output growth with the textile and leather subsector registering a negative 21.1 percent, paper and paper products subsector negative 1.5 percent with the non-metallic mineral products registering a remarkable figure of negative 30.2 percent from the positive figure of 16.3 percent registered in 1990. Zero percent contribution was recorded for the basic metal products subsector with other manufacturing subsectors registering negative 0.7 percent from the 34.0 percent registered in 1990. The outcome resulted in an overall zero percent growth in the sector in 1991. This was a clear indication that the sector growth had completely eroded even before trade liberalization.

3.4 Post-trade liberalization Performance of the Manufacturing Sector

At the onset of trade liberalization in 1992, data in the tables 1.1 and 1.2 showed that the manufacturing sector recorded a significant growth rate of 12.1 percent from the zero growth in 1991. On the other hand, manufacturing sector contribution to GDP grew to 30.2 percent from the constant level of 26.5 percent in 1990 and 1991.

As for the manufacturing subsector performance in 1992, data showed favorable performance in output growth accounted mainly by the food, beverages and tobacco subsector of 25.6 percent with basic metal products and other manufacturing subsectors contributing 13.6 percent and 19.7 percent respectively. Only the fabricated metal products registered a positive contribution of 2.5 percent to output growth, though a decline from the 3.3 percent figure registered in 1991.

Notwithstanding the above, the manufacturing sector started to experience the effects of trade liberalization from 1993 onwards. As could be noted from the table 1.1 above, the manufacturing sector in the period 1993 to 1995 showed unfavorable performance with its contribution to GDP showing a constant but a declined trend. In the period, the sector registered negative growth of negative 7.9 percent in 1993, negative 8.6 percent in 1994 and negative 2.7 percent in 1995 with a constant contribution to GDP of 26.0 percent over the period 1993 and 1995. This was attributable mainly in the fluctuations in subsector growth rates as depicted in table 1.0 above. For instance, 1993 data as contained in table 1.2 depicted that only the wood and wood products and chemicals, rubber and plastic products sub-sectors showed positive output growth of 5.3 percent and 5.1 percent respectively. All other subsectors registered negative output growths. This was the first time that even the food, beverages and tobacco subsector recorded a negative output growth of 2.7 followed by textile and leather industries with negative 28.6 percent, paper and paper products negative 1.8 percent, Non-metallic mineral products negative 9.0 percent, fabricated metal products negative 18.6, with other manufacturing subsector registering a negative 10.2 percent. Only the wood and wood products and chemicals, rubber and plastics products subsectors showed positive output growths of 5.3 percent and 5.1 percent respectively.

The situation was similar for 1994 where the manufacturing sector again recorded a negative growth of negative 8.6 percent from the negative 7.9 percent recorded in 1993. Other than the insignificant growth of 0.6 percent achieved by the paper and paper products subsector, all other subsectors recorded negative growths. The most affected was the non-metallic mineral products subsector which recorded a negative 31.3 percent from the 9.0 percent recorded in 1993. This was followed by the chemical, rubber and plastics subsector with a negative 23.0 percent from the positive growth of 5.1 percent in 1993 with the wood and wood products subsector recording a negative 20.7 percent from negative 18.6 percent in 1993 with other manufacturing subsectors recording negative 10.2 percent from the negative 10.4 percent in 1993. The food, beverages and tobacco, textile and leather products and the basic metal products subsectors recording negative growth rates of 3.5 percent, 6.2 percent and 8.0 percent from the 1993 negative figures of 2.7 percent, 28.6 percent and zero percent output growth respectively.

The trend continued even in 1995 where the manufacturing sector again recorded a negative growth of 2.7 percent from the negative 8.6 percent in 1994. Subsector performance was equally unimpressive as most of the subsectors once again recorded negative growth rates with the paper and paper products recording negative 29.9 percent from the positive 0.6 percent in 1994. The other subsectors recorded negative output growth of 13.0 percent for textile and leather products, 13.1 percent for Wood and wood products, 12.8 percent for chemicals, rubber and plastics with 4.3 for basic metal products and 6.1 percent for other manufacturing products. Only the food, beverages and tobacco, non-metallic mineral products and fabricated metal products subsectors recorded positive output growth of 0.5 percent, 5.8 percent and 5.9 percent respectively. Despite these variations in the subsector output growth, the overall sector contribution to GDP growth remained constant in the period 1993 to 1995 at an average of 26.2 percent, down by 4.0 percent registered in 1992.

3.5   Attributes to the Manufacturing Sector Performance Variations

The sector's variations in its performance in the post-trade liberalization period were mainly attributed to stiff competition resulting from liberalization of external trade. High competition from cheaper imported goods and rising cost of raw materials input emanating from high duty on them greatly contributed to non-competitiveness of local products. As for subsector positivity in output growth, these were attributed to the economic reforms which were undertaken by government in the post-trade liberalization period and included privatization and the liberalization of trade and investment. These reforms helped to improve efficiency and productivity in many sub-sectors thus enabling them to withstand foreign competition. Further, the suspension of duty on some imported industrial inputs provided an impetus to the performance of the sector.

However, there were some inhibiting factors to output expansion in this sector. These included foreign competition and high cost of production. The difficulties in the sale of mining units also negatively affected performance. The difficulties in the completion of the sale of the remaining assets of mining conglomerate also contributed heavily to the decline in the fabricated metal products industry. In addition, declining demand to and from mining compounded decline in the performance of the sector as most manufacturing industries where chain linked to mining activities. There was also the factor of high production costs particularly caused by high utility costs of electricity, petroleum products, water and transport in most of the manufacturing industries. The other factor hinged on the insufficient long-term development finance in the period which adversely affected the performance of the sector. As for the unfavorable performance of the chemicals, rubber and plastics subsector, this was mainly caused by the changes in lines of business by large establishments from manufacturing to trading.

With trade been liberalized in 1992, the manufacturing sector with identifiable challenges in its operations, most of its industries could not cope with the effects of liberalization. The most affected among the manufacturing industries was the textile industry which could not survive under trade liberalization due to competition from imported textile products after the opening up of the economy. The only two textile industries in the country would not manage the effects of liberalization and had to shut down. The main reason for the shut down had to do with financial problems which resulted in them experiencing shortfalls in foreign exchange required to procure the necessary raw materials. The lack of adequate foreign exchange initially only forced them to reduce production but eventually the problem could not be contended forcing them to completely "close shop" (New African, 1993, p26). This was the common trend with many other companies who were found struggling to survive in a liberalized economy. Without private investment bail out, the hopes of survival for most of these industries became bleak. Most potential industries such as Chilanga cement of Zambia were lack to only experience a mere change of ownership of the company. But in case of other companies, this did not happen as only government protectionist interventions were deemed to be necessary for their survival.

3.6   Effects of Trade Liberalization on Manufacturing Sector Employment

The advent of trade liberalization in Zambia brought with it a lot of challenges to the manufacturing sector. This was the time when most of the sector's industries became more exposed to external competition. Without firm economic stability, this made it difficult for most of the industries to contend the effects of liberalization. In some cases, industries with a weaker financial position found it difficult to withstand the competition from the foreign industries and were eventually left with no option but to close down completely. For some, there only option to them was re-location to the neighboring countries where the production costs were perceived to be low. This trend greatly affected the labour market as a result of huge losses in employment following the closure of most of the local manufacturing industries. The major problem of the manufacturing industries was that in the pre-liberalization period, most of the industries in the manufacturing sector were customized to protectionist tendencies being government owned and formed part of the import-substitution sectors of the economy. Arguably, employment levels in most of the industries were higher than economically necessary. The downtrends in the sector's formal employment were clearly indicated in Table 2.0 below.

Table 2.0: Manufacturing Sector Formal Employment 1989-1995

	1989	1990	1991	1992	1993	1994	1995
Total Formal Employment	540,500	543,300	544,200	546,000	520,000	489,800	479,400
Manufacturing Share of Formal Employment	75,200	77,100	75,400	73,600	67,600	57,100	55,654
Percentage Share of Manufacturing Sector to Formal Employment		14.2	13.9	13.5	13.0	11.7	11.6
Changes in Manufacturing Formal Employment		1,900	(1,700)	(1,800)	(6,000)	(10,500)	(1,446)
Percentage Changes of Manufacturing Formal Employment		2.5	-2.3	-2.4	-8.9	-18.4	-2.6

Source: Central Statistics Office

In the table above, the percentage share of the manufacturing sector formal employment to total formal employment showed it to have averaged 13.8 percent in the period 1989 and 1992, but declined to an average of 12.1 percent between 1993 and 1995. The period of the decline was the time of trade liberalization. Between 1989 and 1990, manufacturing share of formal employment was positive with an addition of 1,900 employees representing 14.2 percent share of a manufacturing sector to formal employment. This showed a positive 2.5 percentage change of manufacturing formal employment.

As for the annual analysis, data showed the situation to have deteriorated from 1991 onwards where employment level declined from 77,100 in 1990 to 75,400 in 1991, a difference of 1,700 employees, representing negative 2.3 percent change in manufacturing sector formal employment. This proved a decline of 0.3 percent change of the manufacturing sector share to formal employment from 14.2 percent in 1990, declining to 13.9 percent in 1991. The observable figures in the table showed that the sector continued to experience a gradual decline in employment figures between 1991 and 1992 where the 1991 figure of 75,400 in 1992 declined to 73,600, a difference of 1,800 employees representing a 0.4 percent change in manufacturing sector share of formal sector employment. As to the percentage share of manufacturing sector to total formal employment, this declined to 13.5 percent in 1992 from 13.9 percent in 1991 representing a negative 2.4 percentage change in manufacturing sector formal employment.

The percentage changes in manufacturing sector formal employment were more significant in the period 1992 and 1994 were the sector experienced changes in manufacturing formal employment of 6,000 between 1992 and 1993 and a total of 10,500 between 1993 and 1994. As for the period 1994 to 1995, the sector change in formal employment improved by only 1,446 employees representing percentage changes of manufacturing formal employment of negative 2.4 percent between 1991 and 1992, negative 8.9 percent between 1992 and 1993, negative 18.4 percent between 1993 and 1994 with only negative 2.6 between 1994 and 1995. In terms of percentage changes of the manufacturing share to formal employment, the sector registered negative 0.4 percent in the period 1991 and 1992, negative 0.5 percent in the period 1992 and 1993, negative 1.3 percent in the period 1993 and 1994 with a zero percent in the period 1994 and 1995 clearly showing the effect of liberalization on manufacturing sector formal employment. As explained above, this trend was due to the fact that most of the manufacturing industries could not cope with the effects of liberalization and had to cut down their production capacity or completely closed down.

In the period 1996 up to the time of the 2006 – 2010 Fifth National Development Plan (FNDP), the manufacturing sector performance varied in certain instances showing insignificant growth rates of manufacturing GDP in most of its subsectors. The situation was the same with manufacturing employment share to total formal employment. But due to the limitation of the study, data had to be presented only in a tabulation form. This was clearly indicative in table 3.1 and 3.2 below.

Table 3.1: Manufacturing Sector GDP at Constant 1994 Prices, 1996 -2005 (K' million)

Subsector	Food, Beverage & Tobacco	Textile, leather, & leather products	Wood & wood Products	Paper & paper products	Chemical, Rubber & Plastics	Non-metallic Mineral Products	Basic Metal Products	Fabricated Metal Products	Other Manufacturing	Total Manufacturing	Total GDP	Manufacturing in Total	Changes in Manufacturing
1996	144.3	27.1	18.1	4.8	20.6	4.7	3.1	7.9	0.5	231.10	2,328.10	9.9	0.0%
1997	138.6	39.1	19.6	7.2	22.5	4.1	3.3	8	0.5	242.90	2,404.90	10.1	5.1%
1998	146	42.4	19.2	7.3	18.7	4.5	1.3	7.3	0.5	247.20	2,360.20	10.5	1.8%
1999	154.8	44.8	19.3	7.6	15.5	4.4	1.3	5.9	0.6	254.20	2,412.70	10.5	2.8%
2000	155.7	45.8	19.2	7.5	21.9	4.6	1.4	6.5	0	262.60	2,497.60	10.5	3.3%
2001	164	46.8	20.3	7.8	22.8	4.8	1.2	6	0	273.70	2,619.80	10.4	4.2%
2002	173.8	49.7	21.9	8	25.1	4.9	1.2	5.8	0	290.40	2,706.70	10.7	6.1%
2003	187.7	51.3	24.4	8.6	26.4	5.6	1.4	6.1	0	311.50	2,846.50	10.9	7.3%
2004	198.6	50.3	25.4	8.9	28.6	6.4	1.4	6.4	0	326.00	2,999.30	10.9	4.7%
2005	205.7	48.9	26.3	9.8	29.5	6.9	1.4	6.8	0	335.30	3,159.50	10.6	2.9%

Table 3.2: Manufacturing Sector Employment, 1996 - 2005

Subsector	Total Formal Employment	Manufacturing Share of Formal Employment	Percentage Share of Manufacturing in total Formal Employment	Changes in Manufacturing formal Employment	Percentage Changes in Manufacturing growth rate
1996	479,400	47,400	9.9		
1997	473,161	47,118	10.0	(6,239)	(0.1)
1998	466,925	46,685	10.0	(6,236)	(0.1)
1999	477,503	46,000	9.6	10,578	(0.1)
2000	476,347	47,782	10.0	(1,156)	0.4
2001	475,316	47,679	10.0	(1,031)	(0.0)
2002	437,984	71,705	16.4	(37,332)	5.5
2003	416,804	37,512	9.0	(21,180)	(8.2)
2004	416,228	45,785	11.0	(576)	2.0
2005	436,336	40,151	9.2	20,108	(1.3)

Source: Self Computations

3.7   Government Initiatives in Post-trade Liberalization period 1993 -1995 and beyond

To revitalize the manufacturing sector, Government had to offer incentives to the local manufacturers. This was meant to enhance the competitiveness of the manufacturing sector. In the period 1996 and beyond, the government took steps to enhance productivity in the sector. This was done by providing tax incentives including suspension of duty on raw material imports of selected items and changes in sales tax to value-added tax meant to cushion producers from the double taxation on inputs. In this regard, customs and excise duties on certain inputs were reduced. Further, Government had to undertake measures aimed at improving the business environment in the country. This included the expediting of VAT refunds and implementing measures to stabilize the exchange rate. These measures proved to be positive to the sector.

Specifically, from 1996 up to the period of the FNDP, the transformation of the manufacturing sector and sustainability to competition remained among the major factors that determined the pace of economic activities in Zambia. The manufacturing sector was taken as a pivot of economic development by its backward and forward linkages to economic growth, exports and employment creation. This was because of its provision of a market for primary products and the setting of the basis for exports with employment generation capacity. Policy, institutional and legislative reforms which were undertaken in the period of the FNDP contributed towards a more conducive investment environment for both foreign and domestic investments, including the Micro, Small and Medium Enterprises (MSMEs).

Analysis of the manufacturing sector's contribution to GDP in the FNDP period showed that the share of manufacturing to total exports remained constant in the period at an average of 2.1 percent while its contribution to total formal employment averaged 10.2 percent against the target of 15 percent. In terms of the sector's annual growth, an average of 3.3 percent was achieved against the projected growth of 7.5 percent. Its contribution to total employment increased from 1.3 percent in 2005 to 3.2 percent in 2008 as depicted in Figure 1.0 below.

Figure 1.0: Contributions of Manufacturing Sector 2006-2009

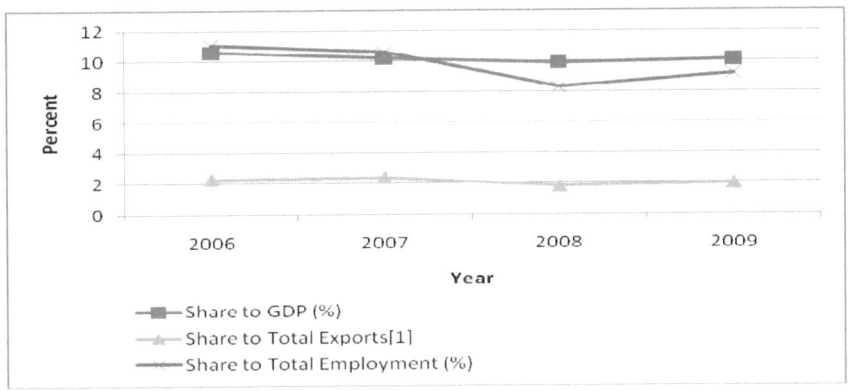

Source: Central Statistics Office, 2010

The growth rate of the manufacturing sector in the same period declined from 5.8 percent in 2006 to 2.5 percent in 2009. The overall decline in the manufacturing sector was due to significant drops in productivity in the textiles and clothing, leather and leather products and fabricated metals sub-sectors. This drop in productivity was largely due to the high cost of doing business; reduced demand for locally produced products and the impact of the global economic crisis as clearly depicted in Figure 2.0 below.

Figure 2.0: Percentage Growth of Manufacturing Sector: 2005-2009

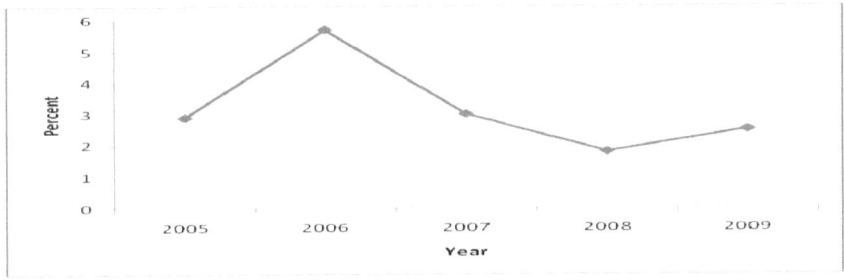

The figure 3.0 below depicted the performance of each sub-sector in terms of percentage changes in their contribution to the manufacturing sector.

Figure 3.0: Percentage Change in Sub-sector Growth to Manufacturing GDP (2005 – 2009)

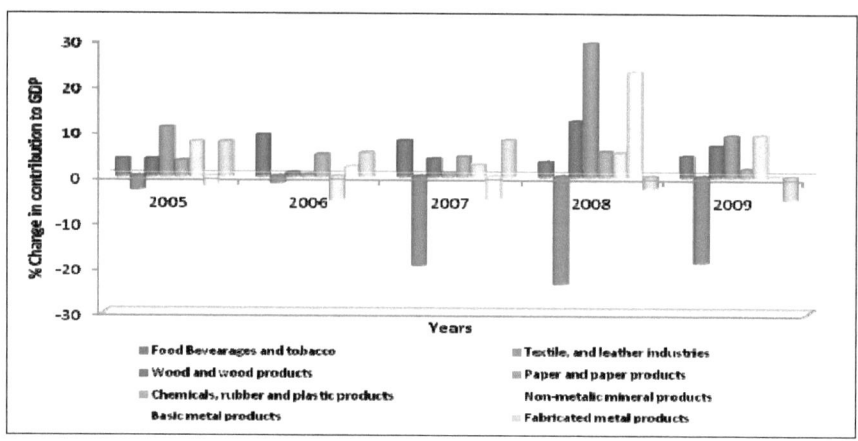

Source: Sixth Nation Development Plan (SNDP)

The study finding was that the significant decline in the textiles and leather products recorded throughout the FNDP period was mainly due to reduced domestic demand in favour of cheap imported textile products from Asian economies. The other thing bordered on the failure of the textiles sub-sector to compete on the regional and international markets thus the reduction of exports. In addition, there was also the issue of increased imports of second hand clothes into the country which further contributed to the problems of the textiles sub-sector. As with the decline in the fabricated metal products, this was mainly attributed to reduced demand of fabricated metals by mining companies due to the economic crisis. The food and beverages sub-sector, on the other hand, experienced growth and sustained its contribution to the total GDP. The sub-sector thrived mainly on account of increased investments resulting from companies expanding their plant and the coming on stream of edible oils processing industries.

Despite improvements in the policy, institutional and legislative frameworks in the FNDP period, the sector still faced a number of challenges. These challenges included the high cost of doing business largely on account of poor physical infrastructure and high production costs, disruptions in power supply, low investments in Research and Development, and obsolete technology. There were also issues of high cost of borrowing, limited standardization and quality assurance and limited human capital and skills required to run the manufacturing industry on a sustainable basis.

4   Government's Options for Manufacturing Sector Growth – The Way Forward

In line with the strategic focus in the SNDP, Government's emphasis has to be on the enhancement of competitiveness of manufacturing through infrastructure and human development. These two factors were found essential as support to the growth of the sector. Further the government needed to accelerate the implementation of the Private Sector Development Reform Programme as a conduit for the growth of the private sector. The issue of Multi-Facility Economic Zones (MFEZ) and Industrial Parks equally need to be reactivated to ensure the development of a vibrant manufacturing industry that takes both foreign and local investors confidence and one that would foster quick economic development by increasing employment opportunities. Further, the manufacturing backward and forward linkages in Energy, Transport, Information and Communications Technology and Agriculture sectors need to be seriously considered. Any other initiatives that the government plans to undertake need serious thought so as not the hamper the already advanced process to the growth of the manufacturing industry.

On the basis of abundance resource endowment, the Government was found with no option but to ensure the acceleration of the expansion programme for the sector so as maximize its potential as a key component to economic growth. The maximization of the sector would lead the country to experience unprecedented increase in economic activities and eventually to the attainment of the national goal of poverty reduction through wealth creation. The sector was found to be a key component to the revitalization of the economy because of its greater potential for both income generation and job creation due to its forward and backward linkages to other sectors of the economy, particularly agriculture and mining. The onus therefore laid on the manner in which the government was to address the identified constraints that posed challenges to the growth of the sector.

5   Conclusion

The study proved that trade liberalization impacted heavily on the manufacturing sector in peak period of its implementation. As for the import substitution policy and the effects of globalization on the growth and development of manufacturing sector, the study also found out these among many other factors attributed to a greater extent to the failure of the manufacturing sector to perform to expectation over the peak period of trade liberalization. However, government policies to cushion itself from the effects of globalization and to revitalize the manufacturing sector proved to have brought about some favorable results despite the many constraints that the sector has had to face over the years of trade liberalization. It therefore remained for the government to continue pursuing policy measures strategically focused on the growth of the sector seriously taking into consideration its backward and forward linkages in the economy.

Bibliography

Chikoti, S. and. Mutonga, C. Q (2002), Textiles and Clothing in Zambia, Ministry of Commerce, Trade and Industry, Lusaka

Economist Southern Africa vol. 3 No. 5, June 1993

Government of the Republic of Zambia (1994), Economic Report, Office of the President, National Commission for Development Planning, Lusaka

Government of the Republic of Zambia (1995), Economic Report, Office of the President, National Commission for Development Planning, Lusaka

Government of the Republic of Zambia (1996), Economic Report, Ministry of Finance and Economic Development, Lusaka

Government of the Republic of Zambia (1997), Economic Report, Ministry of Finance and Economic Development, Lusaka

Government of the Republic of Zambia (1998), Economic Report, Ministry of Finance and Economic Development, Lusaka

Government of the Republic of Zambia (2006), Fifth National Development Plan 2006 – 2010, Ministry of Finance and National Planning, Lusaka

Government of the Republic of Zambia (2007), 2007 Annual Fifth National Development Plan Progress Report, Ministry of Finance and National Planning, Lusaka

Government of the Republic of Zambia (2011), Sixth National Development Plan 2011 – 2015, Ministry of Finance and National Planning, Lusaka

Government of the Republic of Zambia (2004), Poverty Reduction Strategy Paper, Ministry of Finance and National Planning, Lusaka

Government of the Republic of Zambia (2004), Second Poverty Reduction Strategy Paper Implementation Progress Report July 2003 – June 2004, Ministry of Finance and National Planning, Lusaka

Gulhati, R (1989) Impasse in Zambia: The Economics and Politics of Reform, Economic Development Institute, World Bank, Washington D.C

Gweynne, R (1996), 'Trade and Developing Countries'. In Daniels, P.W. and Lever W.F (eds), Global Economy in Transition, Longman, Essex

Koyi, G (2006), The Textile and Clothing Industry in Sub-Saharan Africa: In Herbert Jauch / Rudolf Traub-Merz (Eds.); The Future of the Textile and Clothing Industry in Sub-Saharan Africa, Friedrich-Ebert-Stiftung, Bonn

Kenichi, Ohmae (2005), The Next Global Stage, Challenges and Opportunities in our Borderless World, Wharton School Publishing

Mulungushi, J.S (2007), Policy Development and Implementation in the Post-Liberalization Era in Zambia (1990S and Beyond): Towards a Participatory Planning and Economic Management Model, Doctorate Thesis, University of South Africa

New African, No 310, July 1993

Osei-Hwedie, B.Z (2003), Development Policy and Economic Change in Zambia: A reassessment, DPMN Bulletin: Volume X, No. 2

Seidman A, (1979), The Distorted Growth of Import Substitution: The Zambian Case, in Ben Turok (ed.), Development in Zambia, ZED Press, London

Soderstein, B, (1980), International Economics, MacMillan Education Ltd

Steger, Manfred. B. (Ed) (2003), Globalization: A Very Short Introduction. Oxford University Press

Turok B, (1979), Development in Zambia, Zed Press, London

Watts M, (1992), What is a Market Economy, U.S Information Agency

Wikipedia, (2012), The Free Encyclopedia,

World Bank (1987), World Development Report, Washington D.C

World Bank, (1993), World Economic Outlook, Washington D.C

World Bank, (1992), Trends in Developing Economies, Washington D.C